The Goose That Laid the Golden Eggs
with
The Farmer and His Sons

Illustrated by Val Biro

Award Publications Limited

An old man and an old woman lived in an old house. They were very poor. They had nothing but a white goose.

One day the goose laid an egg.
It had never laid an egg before.
The egg was made of gold!

"It is solid gold!" cried the old man. "We will be the richest people in the village!"
They danced and cheered.

The next day the goose laid another golden egg. But the old man and the old woman became greedy.

"It will take a long time to become rich if we get only one egg a day," said the old woman. "Let's cut open the goose and have all the golden eggs at once!"

So they did just that. But they found that the goose was not filled with golden eggs at all.

The old man and the old woman had been too greedy. Now they had no more golden eggs and no goose.

The Farmer and His Sons

An old farmer had worked hard all his life. He grew big, juicy grapes in his vineyard.

People paid a lot of money for his grapes, but the farmer was not happy. He was worried.

The farmer had three sons.
They were very lazy and never
did any work on the vineyard.

He worried that they would not take good care of the vineyard after he died.

The farmer knew that his sons did not understand the importance of hard work.

One day he had an idea. He told them, "When I am gone, remember that there is a great treasure in my vineyard."

When the farmer died, his sons remembered what he had said. Thoughts of gold, bags of coins, and chests of silver filled their heads.

"We will dig for the treasure!" they cried. They ran to the vineyard with a shovel, a fork and a hoe and set to work.

They dug out every weed to look for pearls underneath. They turned over the hard soil to look for silver coins.

Week after week, the sons worked hard in the vineyard, but they did not find a single coin or nugget of gold.

When they had worked over the last piece of soil they stopped. "Father must have played a trick on us," they said.

Tired from their hard work, the sons fell asleep. They were very disappointed that they had not found any treasure.

But they had dug the vineyard so well that the grapes grew bigger than ever before! When the grapes were ripe, the sons took them to market.

Everybody wanted to buy some of the marvellous grapes. Soon the sons' pockets were full of money.

"The grapes are the treasure in the vineyard!" the sons cried. "If we work hard there will be more treasure next harvest."

The farmer's sons now knew the importance of hard work.